Piano • Vocal • Guitar

# SONGS OF THE 80's

## THE DECADE SERIES

## HAL • LEONARD®
## CORPORATION
7777 W. BLUEMOUND RD. P.O. BOX 13819 MILWAUKEE, WI 53213

Periods in music, unlike decades, rarely arrive fully defined with the countdown to the New Year by Guy Lombardo or Dick Clark. While the new sounds waiting to inevitably supplant the old are generally percolating in the underground by then, it usually takes some time before they gather enough momentum to wash away the entrenched sounds of the previous era. Although it would come to define the Fifties, rock 'n' roll would spend a good five years impatiently gyrating in the nether realms of R&B and Country music, before it mustered the psychic force to push pop music off the radio dial.

In the early Sixties, with the sounds of rock'n' roll still dominating the Top 40, the world was on the brink of a New Frontier, and the true nature of the era was being shaped in the Bohemian underground of Greenwich Village and the red light district of Hamburg, Germany. It wasn't until 1965, when a folkie named Bob Dylan met the Beatles, at the top of the charts, that the sound of folk/rock/protest gained recognition as the musical mirror of those chaotic times. Defining the cooling off period of the Seventies, Disco wiped the slate clean around mid-decade, with its numbing beat obliterating all thoughts and memories of the introspective singer/songwriter.

Thus, what we must determine about the Eighties is not only its musical essence, but when, or indeed if, a defining sound and feeling of the decade ever did arrive.

My premise is, it never did.

Certainly, on the calendar, the profile of the Eighties belongs to Ronald Reagan, who celebrated his inauguration with the release of the 44 Iranian hostages in 1981. (In 1980, the victory of the U.S. hockey team over the highly-favored Soviets in the Olympics was, in retrospect, the beginning of a decade-long recovery of the national pride, which was severely damaged during the turmoil of the Sixties and the pall of the Seventies). With the economy on the upswing, the Eighties represented a time of relative peace and prosperity, an implicit return to the traditional values of the Fifties.

While this translated musically into much of the decade being virtually bereft of a need or a marketplace for music of social or artistic significance, the manufacture, presentation and dissemination of musical products, from digital synthesizers to compact discs, to massive national music networks, ironically developed the sounds themselves into objects of processed perfection that easily surpassed — if not masked — the lack of any individuality in the music itself. In the Eighties, truly, the medium became the message and vice-versa. And nowhere as explicitly as on MTV.

Created in 1981, Music TeleVision can arguably be called the sound of the Eighties, with the added impact of the visual element serving to clinch the deal. Just as the Beatles arrived here on TV courtesy of Ed Sullivan, to rescue a nation from its period of mourning over the assassination of JFK, MTV arrived soon after the rock 'n' roll generation had been stunned by the assassination of John Lennon in 1980, with a message that the music had not died along with one of its revered spiritual leaders.

MTV's primary function (aside from providing an auxiliary source of income for a lot of freelance movie and TV extras and fledgling directors) was certainly in the realms of marketing. Harnessing television's overnight starmaking powers to the catchiness of the three-minute single (and what came to be its recurring repertoire of visual hooks), MTV made instant celebrities of anonymous but recognizably telegenic unknowns, like Madonna, Duran Duran, Cyndi Lauper, Boy George and George Michael, and massive superstars of already proven, and potentially telegenic entities, like Tina Turner, Bruce Springsteen, Rod Stewart and Michael Jackson. Jackson's 1982 album *Thriller,* with its assortment of extravagant videos, was definitely the world's first Made-for-MTV LP, benefitting from such massive exposure to sell over 30 million copies worldwide, more than any other album in history.

Of course, with the advent of MTV's explicit visual nature and 24-hour nationwide proliferation, rock 'n' roll lyrics, which had previously been vaguely tolerated, ignored as gibberish, misunderstood, or simply obscured by the backbeat, came under intense scrutiny. Attacks by parents as well as self-appointed guardians of public morality, quasi-governmental agencies like the Parents Music Resource Center, and the industry itself lead to the most fervent outbreak of rock 'n' roll censorship since the dawning of the Elvis era, when Steve Allen read the lyrics to "Hound Dog" on his TV show and dignitaries from Skitch Henderson and Frank Sinatra to the fathers of ASCAP called for its condemnation.

the movie of the same name, symbolized the transition of its composer Richie, from an R&B stylist with the Commodores, to a mainstream artist of the first order. Already entrenched in the mainstream, Linda Ronstadt's decade journeyed through film music ("Somewhere Out There") to the big band pop of Nelson Riddle, the Mexican music of her heritage, to the Broadway stage in *The Pirates of Penzance.*

MTV's implicit mandate was neither to invent or inspire, but, rather, in the mode of most taped television transmissions, to reinvent and recycle, each year to fill in the new fall lineup with familiar faces. Not surprisingly, the other TV networks soon stepped into line. *Miami Vice* became the first regularly scheduled dramatic program to have a soundtrack, complete with rock songs in the background (sometimes the foreground) of the action — sometimes even inspiring the action. Since 1977's *Saturday Night Fever,* the film industry had been aware of the dramatic power of a well-timed tune; in the Eighties nearly every film, from *Fame* to *Flashdance* to *Dirty Dancing* to *Cocktail,* exploited pop songs in an effort not only to sell itself, but to sell soundtrack albums as well.

Aided by Country music's answer to MTV, the Nashville Network, stars like Kenny Rogers and Dolly Parton crossed over with their tunes, not only to the mass audience, but to the greener pastures of TV and the movies; Kenny in *The Gambler,* a remake of one of his hits, and Dolly in *9 to 5,* for which her title song gained an Oscar nomination. Similarly, one of the biggest ballads of the decade, "Endless Love," by Lionel Richie and Diana Ross, from

Once a veritable fount of the best in pop music, Broadway remained dormant of hit tunes through most of the decade. Until the remarkable upsurge in the later part of the Eighties, with *Phantom of the Opera* and *Les Miserables,* virtually the only hit song to emerge during the period was the ineffable "Memory," from Andrew Lloyd-Webber's *Cats.* Everyone from Barry Manilow to Barbra Streisand recorded this song, recalling a grander era of pop music, when standards could routinely accommodate dozens of competing and often complementary versions.

The theater of the younger generation was clearly MTV, its images indelibly planted in the minds of its observers, and repeated every half hour on the hour: Cyndi Lauper's tragi-comic soap opera vignette for "Time After Time;" Bonnie Tyler's bravura performance on the overwhelming "Total Eclipse of the Heart;" Foreigner's emotional rendering of "I Want to Know What Love Is," accompanied by a gospel choir; the heartthrob emergence of George Michael in Wham's "Wake

Me Up Before You Go Go," and "Careless Whisper" and then on his own with "One More Try;" and Tina Turner's spirited and poignant stroll through the sidewalks of "What's Love Got to Do with It," a hip tour de force that launched not only her comeback but a movie career next to Mel Gibson in *Mad Max.*

Inspired by the technology and the opportunity to instantly reach a wider audience on a daily basis, many veteran acts reached new commercial peaks by reinventing themselves in their own MTV image.

Olivia Newton-John went aerobic in "Physical;" Heart got sexy in "These Dreams;" and Elton John matured in "Candle in the Wind," his ode to the idol of a pre-MTV era, Marilyn Monroe.

If the overriding theme of much of the Eighties seemed to have been the personal profit motive, leading to the Yuppie alphabet — MBA, IRA, BMG, CEO, VCR, etc. — chinks in the armor began showing in the faces of fallen heroes: Wall Street scoundrel Ivan Boesky was convicted of illegal insider trading; Jimmy Swaggart, Jim and Tammy Faye Baker, televangelism's Peter, Paul & Mary, were caught and punished for sins against man, woman and nature; Colonel Oliver North, took the fall for Contragate. And with the gradual transformation of the Russian bear from grizzly to teddy, a certain juggling of the political priorities on the international front began to make its vibrations felt in the music over here.

Starting with Bob Geldof's humanitarian gesture to aid famine victims in Ethiopia, "Do They Know It's Christmas," in 1984 which was duplicated in the U.S. the next year with "We Are the World," the musicians of the world banded together to fight starvation, apartheid, and injustice. In a series of inspirational festivals, musicians began to once again take responsibility for the shape of the world theater. Gradually, outspoken, politically aware performers, like the Police, Tracy Chapman and U2, would truly turn the music around to the ideals left behind in the previous decades.

Yet, between the incomparable bookends of a decade that began with freedom for the U.S. hostages

DON'T WORRY, BE HAPPY
Written & Recorded by
BOBBY McFERRIN

(and bespoke the vulnerability of the Russians) and ended with freedom for nearly all of Eastern Europe, there was a wide yin and yang of experiences. Musically these ranged from the easygoing triple crown Grammy victory of Christopher Cross in 1980 (with "Sailing" as Song and Record of the Year, and Cross himself as New Artist) to the return to rock 'n' roll roots and pride espoused by Joan Jett's "I Love Rock and Roll" and the Airplane's "We Built This City." The decade also encompassed the have-a-nice-day simplicity of Bobby McFerrin's "Don't Worry, Be Happy," the song and the book; the raging have-not anger of rap; and the more traditionally stoic balladeering of "There'll Be Sad Songs (to Make You Cry)" by Billy Ocean.

The tragic irony of John Lennon's death to the tune of "(Just Like) Starting Over," was balanced somewhat by the separate comebacks of his former partners, George Harrison ("Got My Mind Set on You") and Paul McCartney ("Ebony and Ivory" with Stevie Wonder). The phasing out of the vinyl single (soon to be followed by the phasing out of vinyl itself, in favor of cassettes and CDs), symbolized the aging of the youths who had discovered rock 'n' roll. This may have been negated a bit by the presence of so many veteran performers at the top of the charts, from Chicago ("Hard Habit to Break") to the Beach Boys ("Kokomo") to the Airplane ("Sara") to Donnie Osmond ("Soldier of Love"). Even an old Louie Armstrong classic ("What a Wonderful World"), was given new life in the Robin Williams film *Good Morning, Vietnam*. At the same time, in the presence of newcomers like Debbie Gibson, Tiffany, Fine Young Cannibals, Poison, Taylor Dayne, and New Kids on the Block, youthfulness returned to the pop scene in the past few years, with an energy and prominence not heard since the early days of rock 'n' roll.

Without a defining sound of its own, rather a polyglot jumble of nostalgic impulses and influences, the music of the Eighties still managed to define the complexities of the decade, by taking stock and re-evaluating the sounds and the messages of the past thirty years. By decade's end, two of the decade's finest artists were able and willing to put it all together for us. In accomplishing the formidable task of following up his monumental *Thriller*, Michael Jackson didn't do a

Billy Joel's contribution to the literature of songs was comparably striking in "We Didn't Start the Fire," being nothing less than an oral headline history of the thirty years the rock 'n' roll generation has been grappling with, from its infancy to the edge of a powerful maturity.

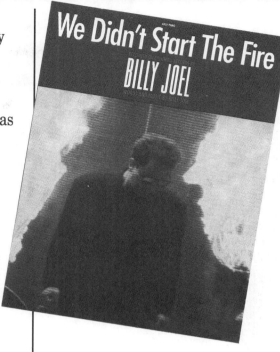

If the Nineties can make use of this idealistic yet informed maturity, couple it with youth's infusion of undefeated energy and vision, and technology's onward rush toward the millennium it should be a time of marvelous music.

*Bad* job at all; from that album, "Man in the Mirror" stands as a tribute and a testament to the artist and the man, reflecting a path toward personal growth and commitment in the new decade.

# CANDLE IN THE WIND

Music by ELTON JOHN
Words by BERNIE TAUPIN

# CARELESS WHISPER

Words and Music by GEORGE MICHAEL
and ANDREW RIDGELEY

# COULD'VE BEEN

Words and Music by
LOIS BLAISCH

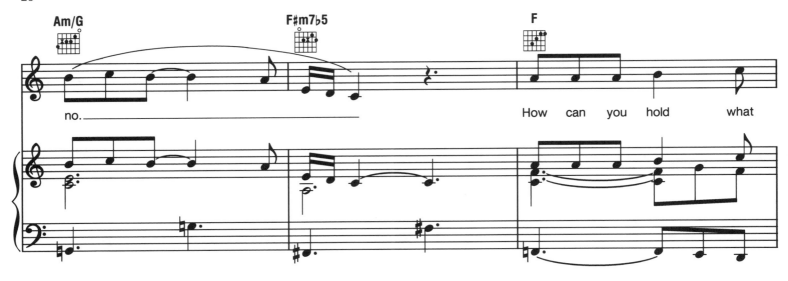

no. How can you hold what

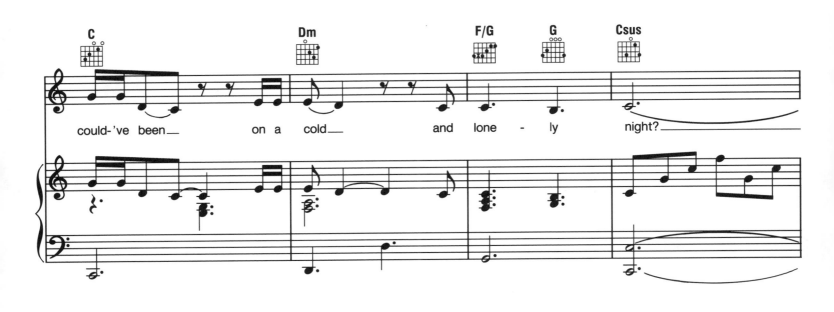

could-'ve been___ on a cold___ and lone - ly night?___

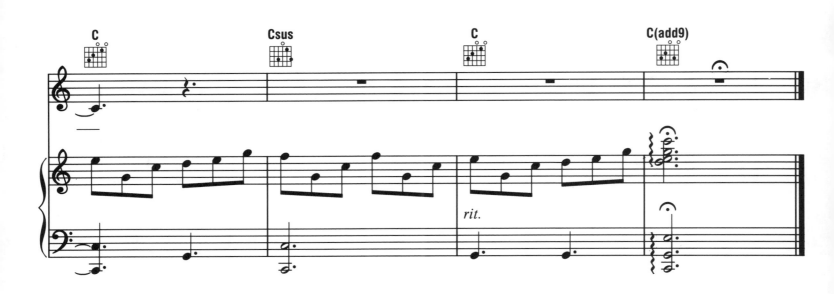

*rit.*

# DON'T WORRY, BE HAPPY

By BOBBY McFERRIN

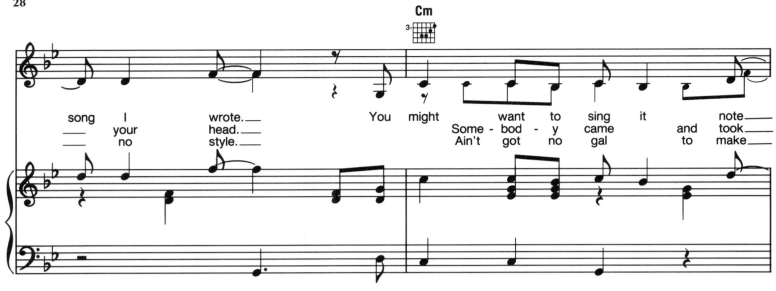

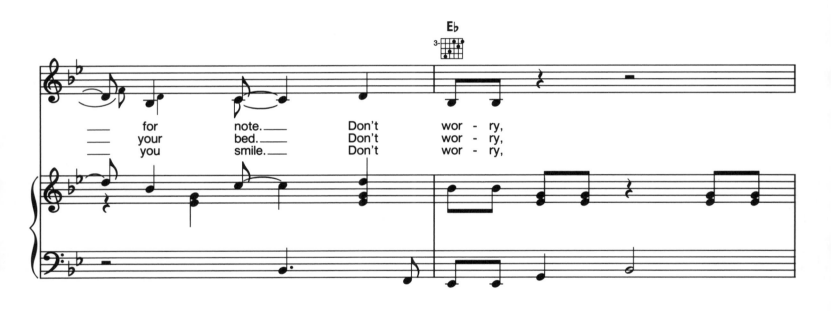

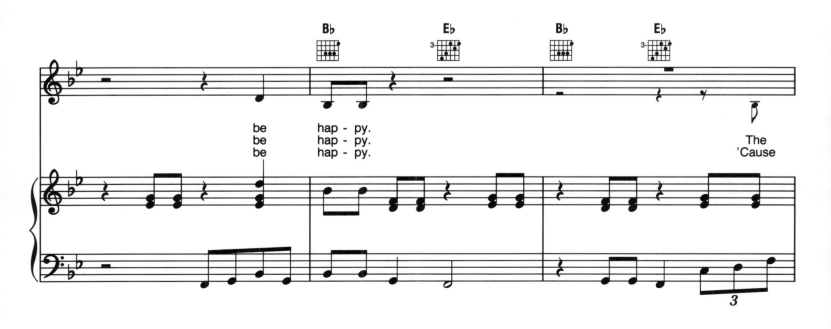

B♭
In ev - 'ry life we have some trou - ble,
land - lord say your rent is late.
when you worry your face will frown.
Cm
but when you wor - ry you make it dou - ble. Don't
He may have to lit - i - gate. Don't
and that will bring ev'ry - bod - y down. Don't
E♭
B♭
E♭
wor - ry, be hap - py. Don't
wor - ry, be hap - py. (Spoken:) Look at
wor - ry, be hap - py. Don't

**Spoken Ad Lib. Over Repeat and Fade:**

Don't worry. Don't worry. Don't do it.
Be happy. Put a smile on your face.
Don't bring everybody down. Don't
worry. It will soon pass, whatever it is.
Don't worry. Be happy. I'm not worried.

I'm happy.

# EBONY AND IVORY

Words and Music by
McCARTNEY

Side by side on my pian - o key - board, oh — Lord, why—

— don't we? _____

**Double tempo**

*Repeat to fade*

E - bo - ny, __ iv - or - y, __ liv - ing in per - fect har - mo - ny. __

# ENDLESS LOVE

Words and Music by
LIONEL RICHIE

41

# EVERY BREATH YOU TAKE

Words and Music by
STING

# EVERY ROSE HAS ITS THORN

Words and Music by B. DALL, C.C. DEVILLE,
B. MICHAELS and R. ROCKETT

We both lie si-lent-ly still_ in the dead of the night._ Al-though we

both lie close to-geth-er,_ we feel miles a-part_ in-side._ Was it

some-thing I said or some-thing I did? Did my words not come out right?_ Though I

# FAST CAR

Words and Music by
TRACY CHAPMAN

# FLASHDANCE . . . WHAT A FEELING

Lyric by KEITH FORSEY and IRENE CARA
Music by GIORGIO MORODER

# GOOD THING

Words by ROLAND GIFT
Music by DAVID STEELE

(Good thing)

# GOT MY MIND SET ON YOU

Words and Music by
RUDY CLARK

# HARD HABIT TO BREAK

Moderately slow

Words and Music by JOHN LEWIS PARKER
and STEVE KIPNER

# I LOVE ROCK 'N ROLL

Words and Music by ALAN MERRILL
and JAKE HOOKER

saw him danc - ing there ___ by the rec - ord ma - chine.
smiled, so I got up ___ and asked ___ for his name.

84

# I'LL ALWAYS LOVE YOU

Words and Music by
JIMMY GEORGE

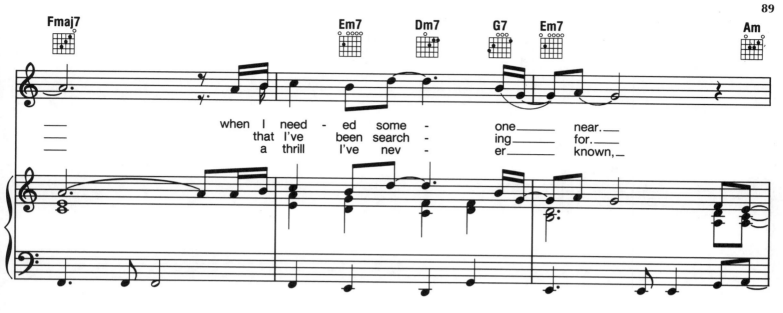

when I need - ed some - one____ near.____
that I've been search - ing____ for.____
a thrill I've nev - er____ known,____

You bring me hap - pi - ness____ ev - 'ry
You are my ev - 'ry - thing.____ Tell me,
and filled my ea - ger heart____ with a

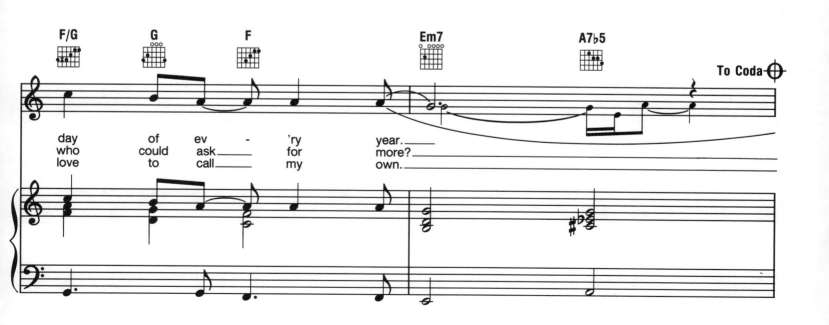

day of ev - 'ry year.____
who could ask____ for more?____
love to call____ my own.____

# I WANT TO KNOW WHAT LOVE IS

Words and Music by
MICK JONES

# I'LL BE LOVING YOU
## (FOREVER)

Words and Music by
MAURICE STARR

# ISLANDS IN THE STREAM

Moderately Slow Rock

Words and Music by BARRY GIBB,
MAURICE GIBB and ROBIN GIBB

# KOKOMO

Words and Music by MIKE LOVE, TERRY MELCHER,
JOHN PHILLIPS and SCOTT McKENZIE

Moderately bright

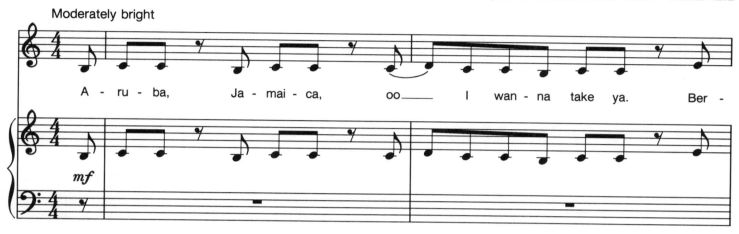

A - ru - ba, Ja - mai - ca, oo____ I wan - na take ya. Ber -

mu - da, Ba - ha - ma, come___ on, pret - ty ma - ma. Key Lar - go, Mon - te - go, Ba -

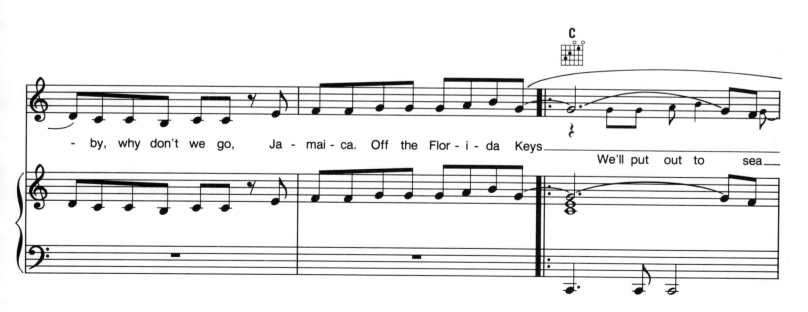

- by, why don't we go, Ja - mai - ca. Off the Flor - i - da Keys____
We'll put out to sea____

# LOST IN YOUR EYES

Words and Music by
DEBORAH GIBSON

# MAN IN THE MIRROR

Words and Music by GLEN BALLARD
and SIEDAH GARRETT

121

# MEMORY
## (From "CATS")

Music by Andrew Lloyd Webber
Text by Trevor Nunn after T.S. Eliot

# MIAMI VICE

**(Theme from the Universal Television Series)**

By JAN HAMMER

**MCA MUSIC PUBLISHING**

# ONE MORE TRY

Words and Music by
GEORGE MICHAEL

(1.) I've had e-nough of dan - ger, and peo-ple on _ the streets,_

[2°] [bye.]

I'm look-ing out for an - gels, just trying to find_ some_peace.

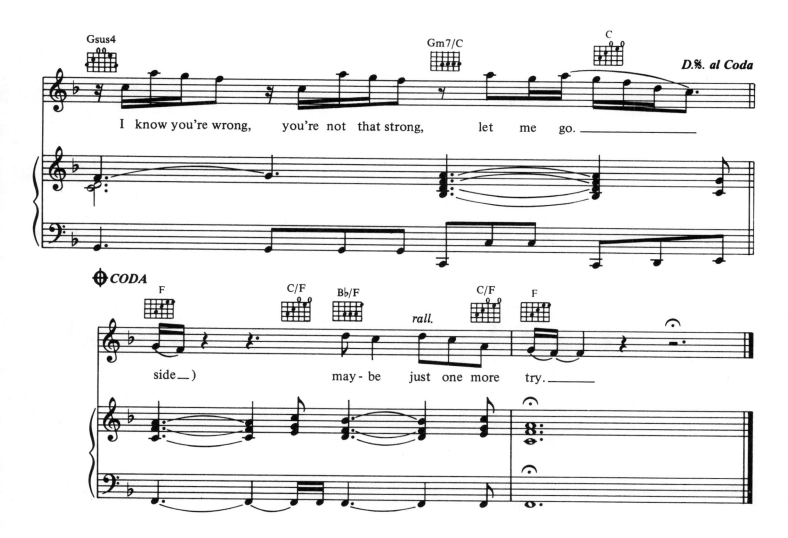

**VERSE 2:**
When you were just a stranger
And I was at your feet
I didn't feel the danger
Now I feel the heat
That look in your eyes
Telling me no
So you think that you love me
Know that you need me
I wrote the song, I know it's wrong
Just let me go . . .

**D.S.**
And teacher
There are things
That I still have to learn
But the one thing I have is my pride
Oh so I don't want to learn to
Hold you, touch you
Think that you're mine
Because there ain't no joy
For an uptown boy
Who just isn't willing to try
I'm so cold
Inside.

# PHYSICAL

Words and Music by STEPHEN A. KIPNER
and TERRY SHADDICK

# Sailing

Words and Music by
CHRISTOPHER CROSS

Well, it's not ___ far down ___ to par - a - dise, at least it's not ___ for me. ___ And if the wind ___ is right ___ you can sail ___ a - way ___ and find tran - quil - i - ty. Oh, the can -

# SARA

Music by PETER WOLF and INA WOLF
Words by INA WOLF

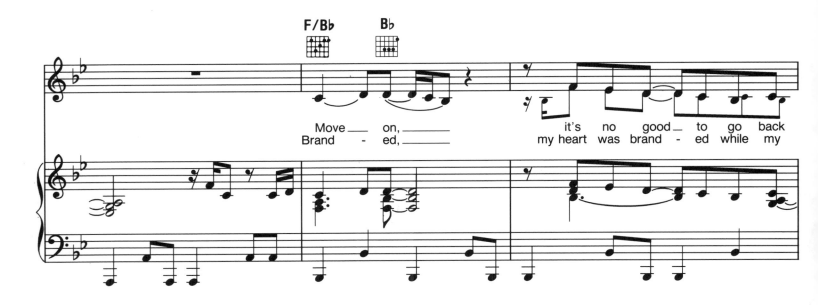

156

# SHE'S LIKE THE WIND

Slowly

Music and Lyrics by PATRICK SWAYZE
and STACY WIDELITZ

She's like the wind____ through my tree.

She rides the night____ next to me. She

leads me through moon - light on - ly to burn____ me with the sun. She's

# SOLDIER OF LOVE

Words and Music by CARL STURKEN
and EVAN ROGERS

**MCA MUSIC PUBLISHING**

# SOMEWHERE OUT THERE
## (From "An American Tail")

By JAMES HORNER, BARRY MANN
and CYNTHIA WEIL

Moderately, with expression

Some - where____ out there be - neath the pale moon - light____ some - one's think - in' of me and

# (JUST LIKE)
# STARTING OVER

Words and Music
by JOHN LENNON

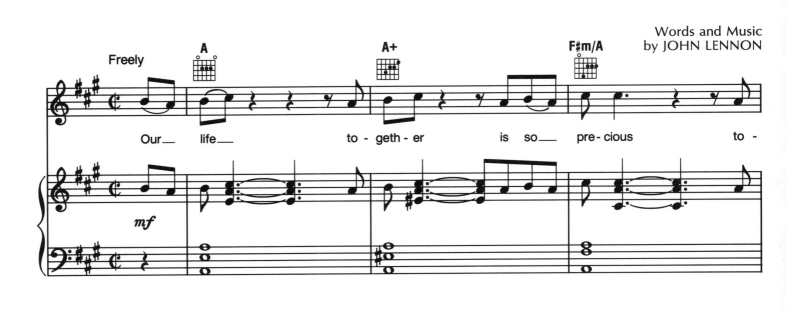

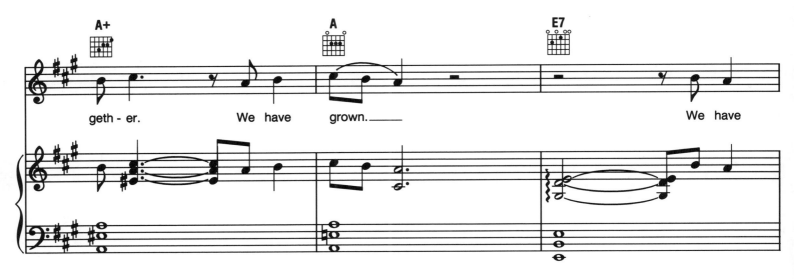

# THERE'LL BE SAD SONGS
## (TO MAKE YOU CRY)

Slow Rock Ballad

Words and Music by WAYNE BRATHWAITE,
BARRY J. EASTMOND and BILLY OCEAN

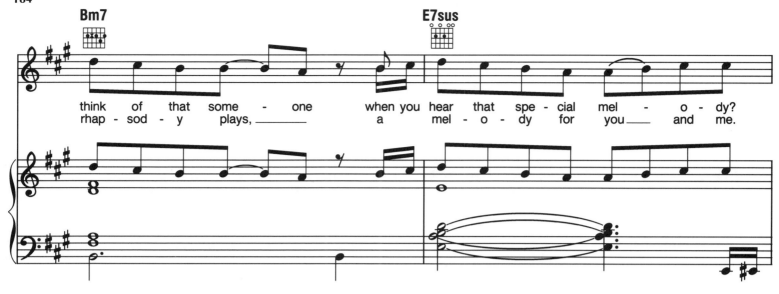

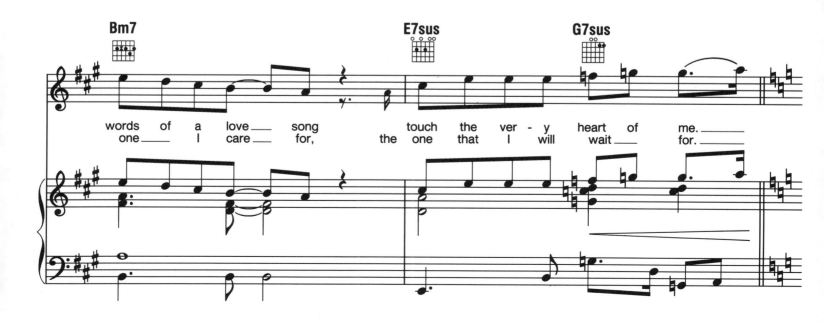

There'll be sad songs to make you cry; __ love __ songs of - ten

do. __ They can touch __ the heart __ of some-one new, __

say - ing I love you. I love you. __

# THESE DREAMS

Words and Music by MARTIN PAGE
and TAUPIN

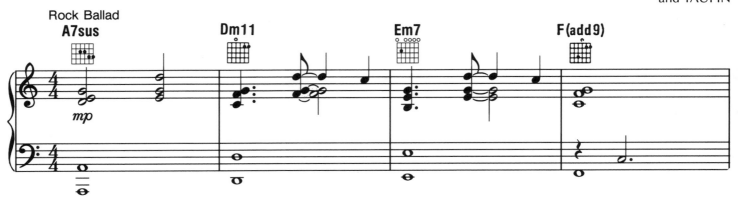

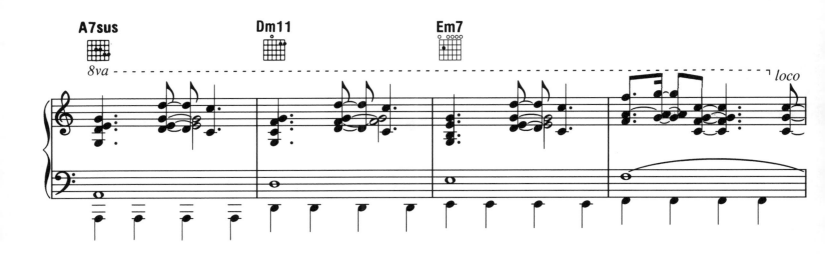

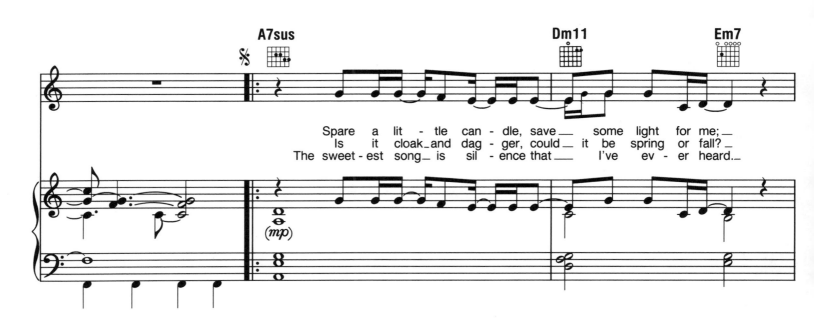

Spare a lit-tle can-dle, save__ some light for me;__
Is it cloak__ and dag-ger, could__ it be spring or fall?__
The sweet-est song__ is si-lence that__ I've ev-er heard.__

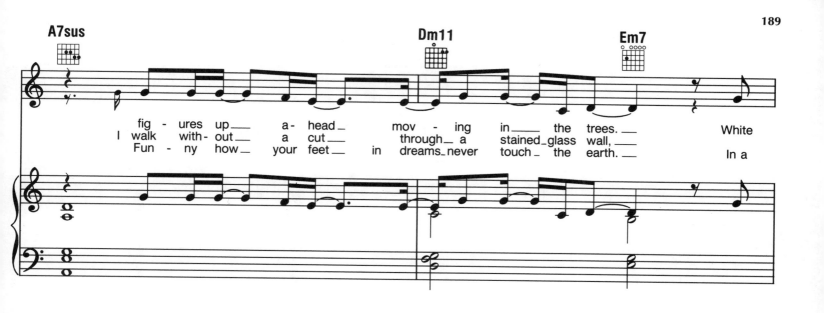

fig - ures up___ a - head___ mov - ing in___ the trees. ___
I walk with - out___ a cut___ through___ a stained glass wall, ___
Fun - ny how___ your feet___ in dreams never touch___ the earth. ___
White
In a

skin in lin - en, per - fume on___ my wrist, ___ and a
weak - er in___ my eye - sight, can - dle in___ my grip, ___ and
wood full of princ - es free - dom is___ a kiss, ___ but the

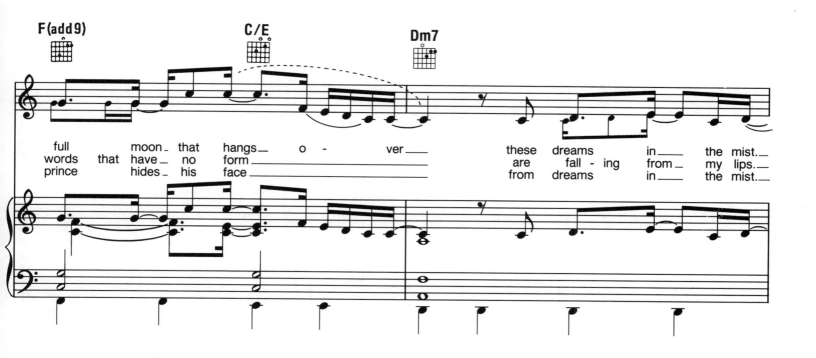

full moon___ that hangs___ o - ver ___ these dreams in___ the mist. ___
words that have___ no form ___ are fall - ing from___ my lips. ___
prince hides___ his face ___ from dreams in___ the mist. ___

# TOTAL ECLIPSE OF THE HEART

Words and Music by
JIM STEINMAN

**Verse 3:**

Turn around
Every now and then I know you'll never be the boy you always wanted to be
Turn around.
But every now and then I know you'll always be the only boy who wanted me the way that I am
Turn around.
Every now and then I know there's no-one in the universe as magical and wonderous as you
Turn around.
Every now and then I know there's nothing any better there's nothing that I just wouldn't do

**Chorus:**

Turn around bright eyes
Every now and then I fall apart
Turn around bright eyes
Every now and then I fall apart

**Middle:**

And I need you now tonight, and I need you more than ever
And if you'll only hold me tight we'll be holding on forever
And we'll only be making it right cause we'll never be wrong together
We can take it to the end of the line.
Your love is like a shadow on me all the time
I don't know what to do and I'm always in the dark
We're living in a powder keg and giving off sparks
I really need you tonight, forever's gonna start tonight, forever's gonna start tonight
Once upon a time I was falling in love, but now I'm only falling apart
Nothing I can do, a total eclipse of the heart
Once upon a time there was light in my life, but now there's only love in the dark
Nothing I can say, a total eclipse of the heart
A total eclipse of the heart

Turn around bright eyes
Turn around bright eyes
Turn around.

# THROUGH THE YEARS

Words and Music by STEVE DORFF
and MARTY PANZER

# TIME AFTER TIME

Words and Music by CYNDI LAUPER
and ROB HYMAN

Moderately Fast Rock

Ly - in' in___ my bed I hear___ the clock tick___ and think of you,___

caught up___ in cir - cles con - fu - sion___ is noth - ing new.___

# WE BUILT THIS CITY

Words and Music by TAUPIN, MARTIN PAGE,
PETER WOLF and DENNIS LAMBERT

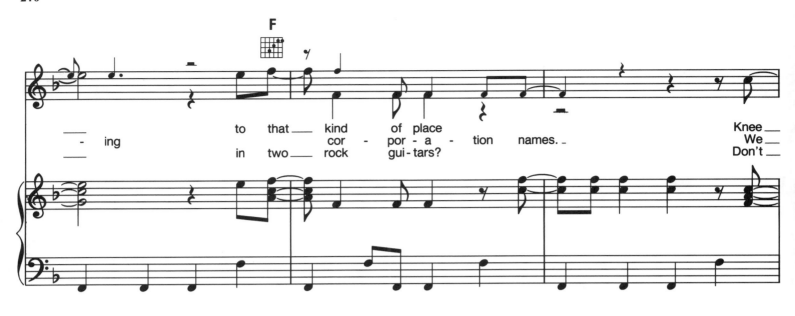

to that ___ kind of place
in two ___ rock gui - tars?

Knee ___
We ___
Don't ___

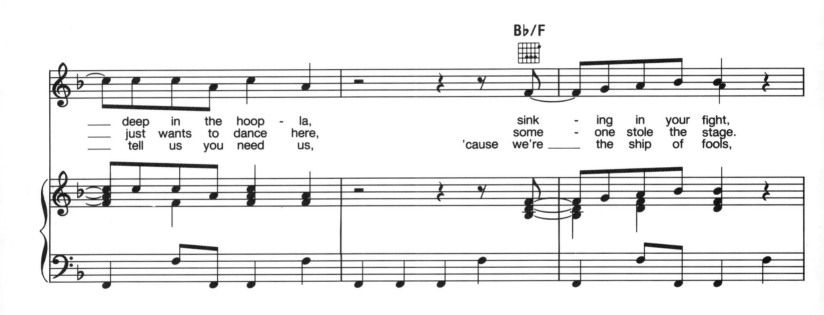

___ deep in the hoop - la,
___ just wants to dance here,
___ tell us you need us,

sink - ing in your fight,
some - one stole the stage.
'cause we're ___ the ship of fools,

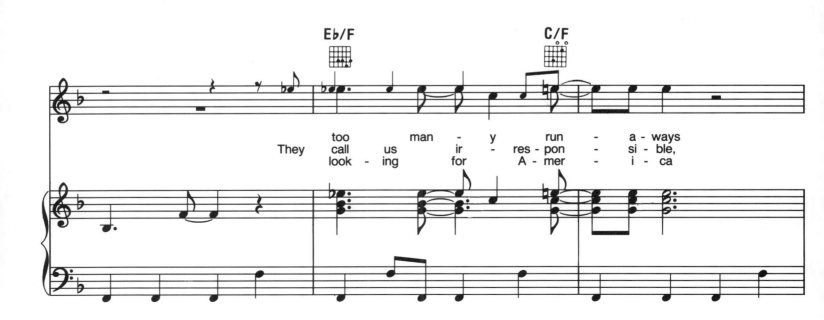

too man - y run - a - ways
They call us ir - res - pon - si - ble,
look - ing for A - mer - i - ca

# WE DIDN'T START THE FIRE

Words and Music by
BILLY JOEL

# WHAT A WONDERFUL WORLD

Words and Music by GEORGE DAVID WEISS
and BOB THIELE

# WAKE ME UP BEFORE YOU GO-GO

Words and Music by GEORGE MICHAEL

# WHAT'S LOVE GOT TO DO WITH IT

Words and Music by TERRY BRITTEN
and GRAHAM LYLE

# WITH OR WITHOUT YOU

Words by BONO
Music by U2